Kerry Murphy
and Fifi Benham

Series editor
ALISTAIR
BRYCE-CLEGG

fantastic ideas for
supporting neurodiversity

BLOOMSBURY

BLOOMSBURY EDUCATION
Bloomsbury Publishing Plc
50 Bedford Square, London, WC1B 3DP, UK
29 Earlsfort Terrace, Dublin 2, Ireland

BLOOMSBURY, BLOOMSBURY EDUCATION and the Diana logo are trademarks
of Bloomsbury Publishing Plc

First published in Great Britain, 2023 by Bloomsbury Publishing Plc
This edition published in Great Britain, 2023 by Bloomsbury Publishing Plc

A catalogue record for this book is available from the British Library

ISBN: PB: 978-1-8019-9218-3; ePDF: 978-1-8019-9216-9

2 4 6 8 10 9 7 5 3 1

Design concept by Lynda Murray
Design by Jeni Child

Printed and bound in India by Replika Press Pvt. Ltd

To find out more about our authors and books visit www.bloomsbury.com
and sign up for our newsletters

Acknowledgements
With special thanks to Sarah Doyle, Tracey Murphy, Ella Kwan and Reia Kwan

Contents

Introduction

When we were asked to write *50 Fantastic Ideas for Supporting Neurodiversity*, we felt mindful that many neurodivergent and disabled children experience interventions that can predominately be adult-directed or prescriptive. This can lead to practice that focuses on training the child out of their neurodivergence or disability. And so, we wanted to offer ideas, but we also wanted to ensure that this book took a neurodiversity-informed and affirming approach. We wanted to produce a book that embraced the concept of fantastic ideas but one which also honours the child's unique way of being.

Our use of neurodivergent is an umbrella term encompassing people who process, learn, and/or behave differently from what would be considered typical. Autism, Attention Deficit Hyperactivity Disorder (ADHD) and dyslexia are specific diagnoses generally considered as neurodivergence; this is not an exhaustive list, as many other disabilities also cause lifelong neurological and physical differences. In Early Years, most children will not have a diagnosis despite observable differences from neurotypical peers. Neurodivergent is, therefore, a useful term to acknowledge children whose needs may not be met adequately by standard practice. We refrain from using the term 'special needs' as we all have a range of access needs, and disabled people's access needs being less likely to be met can be exacerbated by implying their needs are 'special' or 'additional'. The amount of support different neurodivergent children will require in order to have their access needs met will vary, so in this book we address both high- and low-support needs.

It is essential that neurodivergent children are recognised as having unique needs, preferences and strengths with as much variation therein as neurotypical children.

These ideas are intended as a guide for practitioners looking to improve their neurodivergent inclusive practice. Not all suggestions will apply or appeal to every neurodivergent child, so building individual relationships and being able to adapt practice in the moment are key.

As Early Years practice covers a range of settings and roles, the practicality of different activities will vary. Ratios, resources and the space available all impact how to achieve best practice, so activities can be adapted based on these factors. There are always multiple ways to meet the same need and to create the same play opportunities.

You will also notice that we have offered ideas that relate to the process of capturing information about children. We recognise that each local area will be subject to different policies and procedures, and you may need to adhere to these to access support and funding. However, these ideas are there to re-frame some of our thinking and should assist in building positive partnerships with children, families and specialists.

Neurodivergent children may respond to or engage with activities in a way that is unexpected. There is no right or wrong way to play. Children must be given the freedom and support to fully explore their own ideas regardless of whether those ideas follow the practitioner's plan.

We hope that amongst these pages, you find some inspiration and hope in the fact that our neurodivergent and disabled children are competent, capable, unique and worthy of identity-affirming practice.

Both Fifi (they/them) and Kerry (she/her) have lived experience of neurodivergence, and so this book is in part informed by our own ways of being.

Foreword

Fifi Benham and Kerry Murphy's book is a valuable contribution that benefits children who are neurodivergent or have disabilities. The book offers practical ideas that provide guidance and permission to break away from the widely held 'deficit lens' that has been harmful to so many children. By challenging the prevailing notion of what is considered 'normal' and encouraging a more inclusive perspective, the authors are promoting a more equitable and compassionate approach to supporting children's development. The impact of their work has the potential to change the educational experiences of countless children and families, and fully embraces neurodiversity-affirming approaches in early childhood.

David Cahn (ADHD) Free to Learn Childminding

How to use this book

The pages are all organised in the same way. Before you start any activity, read through everything on the page so that you are familiar with the whole activity and what you might need to plan in advance.

What you need lists the resources needed for each activity. Some activities do not require resources.

Definition describes new concepts and ideas that you may not have encountered.

What to do provides both step-by-step instructions and ways in which the overall idea could be implemented.

Neurodiversity-affirming element gives clear guidance on why the idea is neurodiversity affirming. This is in part because many existing strategies and techniques are not underpinned by a neurodiversity approach.

What's in it for the children? outlines the rationale for the idea, and highlights why it is important.

Taking it forward provides extensions to the activities, including how the idea might be expanded, how to work with parents and carers or specialists, or how to build into goal planning for the child's outcomes.

Top tips give a brief word of advice or helpful tip that could make all the difference to how the children experience the activity.

Health & Safety is only included if there are particular issues to be noted and addressed, above and beyond usual health and safety measures

Forms and templates that accompany the activities are available to download from the Bloomsbury Education website: bloomsbury.pub/50-fantastic-ideas-supporting-neurodiversity.

Celebratory one-page profile
Celebrate strengths, interests, differences and needs

What you need:
- Access to PowerPoint or a scrapbook

ALL ABOUT ME

Picture | Basic Information
1. Name: Leo
2. Age: 3
3. Neurotype: Autism

Strengths & Interests | Traits
- Loves Superheroes
- Dancing to Elvis
- Eager to give things a go (with support)
- Talks lots including info bombing about interests

- Immerses himself in play for long periods
- High empathy for animals
- Repeats favourite phrases

Support Needs
- Support with transitions and switching tasks. Leo takes time to move to adult-directed activities.
- Emotional support including knowing his different energy levels and how to respond.
- Peer play, including social relatedness, i.e. knowing how social rules can differ and finding a way to 'meet in the middle'.

What's in it for the children?
During your time with a child, you will develop a wealth of knowledge about their developmental differences and needs. A one-page profile captures all the important information on a single piece of paper through key headings. It is useful for children with a diagnosis whose neurotype or disability might be subject to stereotypes and misconceptions.

Taking it forward
- Create your own one-page profile for children and families before you meet.
- Over time, support the child to take responsibility for their own one-page profile so that they can begin to take ownership of describing and advocating for themselves.

What to do:
1. A one-page profile can be designed in any way you prefer. You might consider using PowerPoint, or you could complete it alongside the child or family on a scrapbook page.
2. Provide *'Basic information'*, including name(s), gender identity, pronouns and neurotype/need. You might also include a picture.
3. Create a heading and write about main *'Strengths and interests'*.
4. Include a heading called *'Traits'*. If the child has a diagnosis, this is where you can emphasise their unique traits rather than focusing purely on delays and deficits. For example, an autistic child may have a preference for solitary or parallel play.
5. Add the heading *'Support needs'*, where you can list the key things the child needs. For example, the child may require Makaton to communicate.

Neurodiversity-affirming element
The profile captures all key 'need to know' information in one place, making it an easy way to quickly gather and share information to ensure consistency of care.

Communication identity

Capturing communication beyond speech

What you need:

- Access to word processing software

What's in it for the children?

All children communicate in various ways, such as body language, signs, visuals or vocalisations. We must honour and seek to understand all forms of communication. It is important not to assume the same behaviours, body language or vocalisations mean the same thing to everyone. There are some neurodivergent children whose external communication directly opposes what they want to express, so providing as many tools as possible for deliberate, meaningful communication is essential.

Taking it forward

- Use this tool to inform decisions about provision. For example, if a child's communication identity is non-speaking, ensure there are environmental supports provided.

What to do:

1. The information can be captured in any way you prefer, for example, using a template or PowerPoint.

2. Choose headings that are relevant to the child. Examples might include:

   - Name and personal meaning

   - Languages spoken

   - Main forms of communication and personal meanings – for example, pointing

   - Things that might get lost in translation

   - Types of interaction that provide comfort

3. Complete this activity together with family, and use the information to inform your practice.

Neurodiversity-affirming element

This tool supports neurodiversity-affirming practice and helps us to honour all communication forms beyond speaking. It helps us to connect with the child and family during transitions and embraces the different funds of knowledge children bring to the setting, as well as ensuring that we meet the different communication needs of all children.

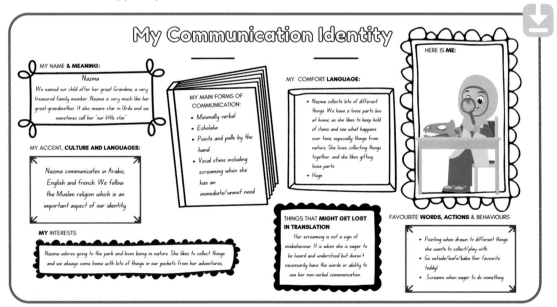

My way to a good day
Support with referral

What you need:

- Access to word processing software, such as Word or Pages

What to do:

1. Rather than thinking about the 'worst days', think about what makes a child's day good. What helps them to thrive, to engage and to learn? Note these under the heading 'What does a good day look like?'.

2. Think realistically about what things need to be in place for a good day. For example, the child might need particular resources to engage, such as fidget toys or noise-cancelling headphones. Note this under the heading 'What might I need to have a good day?'. Here, you can begin to think about what you can and cannot provide.

3. Consider the risks that can hinder a day from being good. For example, if a child cannot communicate their needs due to a lack of visual support. Note these down under the heading 'What are the risks to a good day?'.

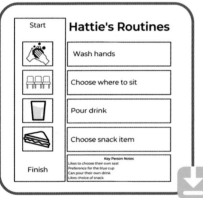

What's in it for the children?

It is quite common to be told to describe children on their 'worst days' when seeking support for developmental differences. While the intention is to highlight how significant the child's needs are, it can also focus on the child as a problem to be fixed. This activity helps to switch the narrative from problem to potential.

Taking it forward

- Use this framework when talking with parents and carers.

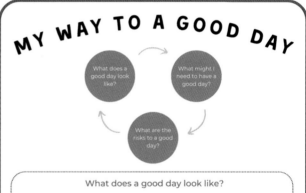

MY WAY TO A GOOD DAY

What does a good day look like?

What might I need to have a good day?

What are the risks to a good day?

What does a good day look like?
- Hattie enjoys quality time with her key person away from the main room, especially when it gets busy and noisy.
- Hattie loves the outdoors, especially risky play. She loves jumping and spinning.
- Being self-directed and able to complete her routines with an element of sameness.

What might I need to have a good day?
- The key person is currently trying to ensure that there are small bursts of 1:1 time outside the main space to play and spend time together. This supports Hattie's emotional regulation and increases her engagement when back in the main room.
- Free flow to the outdoors when possible.
- We are using visuals and sequences to maintain the sameness in routines.

What are the risks to a good day?
Hattie does not like to feel contained in the main playroom as she can become overwhelmed and dysregulated. Elected time out with a key person is important. When she does not have access to this, going outdoors and her routines, it impacts her wellbeing and learning experiences. These outlets optimise her learning, and so adaptions are a must.

Play dictionary
Honouring neurodivergent ways of playing

What you need:

- A notepad
- A pen

What's in it for the children?

It has been suggested that play does not come naturally to neurodivergent and disabled children. This is not necessarily true, and it is becoming more apparent that the way children play can be diverse and may require us to take more time to 'tune in and zoom in' to their unique ways of playing. This activity empowers you to build up knowledge about diverse types of play over time so that children are better understood and supported. When observing a child at play, if there are aspects that you do not yet understand, it might be helpful to use your play dictionary to look for patterns in their play.

Taking it forward

- Use your knowledge of individual children to make the wider environment more inclusive of neurodivergent and disabled play styles.

- Embrace all forms of play to facilitate strength-based discussions with families that show you value and understand their child's differences.

Top tip ⭐

Often, children are taken into adult—led interventions, which can interfere with and deprive them of their play. Instead, let the child take the lead. We can see their perspectives in play more easily if we follow their interests.

What to do:

1. Observe the child and note down the different aspects of their diverse play, especially if they do not yet make sense to you.

2. You might note down things such as:

   - Areas, toys and resources of interest, or things they return to.

   - Repetitive behaviours or actions, including self-stimulatory behaviours.

   - The context – for example, solitary, parallel or cooperative play.

   - Vocalisations, language or forms of communication used.

   - Neurodivergent or disabled styles of play or traits.

3. Over time, you should build a picture of the play interest and develop a deeper understanding of what is happening. This will enable you to lean into the diverse playing style and plan for it as it unfolds.

Neurodiversity-affirming element

Historically, there has been a tendency to believe that neurodivergent or disabled play styles are symptoms rather than traits. There were attempts to eliminate rather than understand play that looked different. Using the dictionary empowers you to look beyond typical play. Child-led play has a wealth of benefits for neurodivergent and disabled children, and by planning based on their unique interests, we honour and support divergent pathways.

PLAY DICTIONARY

Not all play will make sense to you, and it may not "look" conventional. The key is to look beyond typical play, and to think about the diverse features of play:

- Are there any forms of repetition in their play?
- Do they return to particular areas?
- Do they have a fascination with particular objects (remember that these can appear "quirky", for example, rotating door handles)?
- Have you mistaken a form of play for misbehaviour? for example, appearing to destroy or throw things?
- How do they react to the space, for example, sensory seeking or using a particular body part a lot?

Possible Play	Possible Provision	Role of the Adult	Emerging Interests & Extensions

Whole-body affirmations
Celebrating divergent ways of listening and engaging

What you need:
- Affirmation cards

Definition

Whole-body listening is the ability to pay attention and listen in neurotypical ways, such as sitting still, providing eye contact and not fidgeting. This expectation is considered harmful to neurodivergent and disabled children who often pay attention and listen in a diverse range of ways.

Top tip ⭐

It is important to remember that a common neurodivergent trait is self-stimulatory behaviours, known as stimming. This is natural and expected.

What's in it for the children?

This idea provides ways of affirming whole-body communication over whole-body listening, and recognises that children pay attention, listen and engage in a range of ways that can still be considered successful. The use of these affirmations reminds us to honour neurodiversity, and to avoid misinterpreting neurodivergent traits as disruptive.

Taking it forward

- Encourage the children to share their own affirmations, and engage in collaborative activities to establish rules and expectations. When children feel a sense of autonomy and ownership of the environment and expectations, they are more likely to engage.

What to do:

1. Before the activity, create your affirmation cards, similar to the visuals shown.

2. Sit comfortably with the children. Explain that you are going to talk about the different ways you communicate with each other, using cards to help.

3. Talk through each card, and ask the children how each rule might make them feel.

4. Talk to them about the alternative ways in which they pay attention and why it might benefit them to learn and engage.

Neurodiversity-affirming element

By honouring whole-body communication, you are embracing that children engage in listening and attention in different ways, and you are ensuring a greater level of participation by expanding your expectations.

WHOLE BODY AFFIRMATIONS

My body belongs to me!

The only way to understand my body is to be able to make choices about my body.

WHOLE BODY AFFIRMATIONS

I like to move it, move it!

Moving helps me to think including fidgeting and changing positions

WHOLE BODY AFFIRMATIONS

I don't learn to sit still by sitting still...

Sitting comfortably is more important than sitting completely still.

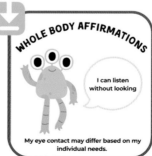

WHOLE BODY AFFIRMATIONS

I can listen without looking

My eye contact may differ based on my individual needs.

WHOLE BODY AFFIRMATIONS

My hands are loud and proud

My hand movements are a valid form of communication.

What you need:

- Odd socks of different colours and patterns

DOUBLE EMPATHY

The story of the odd socks

What's in it for the children?

For a long time, research has focused on describing autistic children as having deficits in their communication, social skills and empathy. Double empathy (Milton, 2012) offers a different theory, whereby the idea is that communication goes both ways, so rather than viewing it as a deficit in the autistic child, it is instead an issue of miscommunication between autistic and non-autistic children. By adopting the use of neuroprops, this double empathy problem can be addressed.

Taking it forward

- Build neurodiversity-informed practice into your everyday practice by listening to and learning from neurodivergent and disabled people.

What to do:

A good way to teach children about neurodiversity is through the use of props that emphasise differences. For example, using socks or selecting a favourite toy to discuss how different children need different things to learn, play and interact.

1. Gather together a selection of odd socks with different colours and patterns.

2. Ask the children to select a sock that appeals to them.

3. Talk to the children about the commonalities and differences between the socks – for example, different colours, patterns and features.

4. Explain that this is how our brains, bodies and personalities works – we each are unique and have different ways of being.

5. Emphasise that all socks are still valuable, just like brains.

Neurodiversity-affirming element

Neurodiversity relates to us all, and so our practice must encompass how all children can connect and begin to understand each other. For example, some children will provide eye contact during interactions whereas other children may feel more comfortable focusing on another part of the person.

WE ALL WEAR DIFFERENT SOCKS

Choose your favourite socks to learn about some of our differences

Definition

The **double empathy problem** is when two children find it hard to understand each other's communication, feelings and thoughts. It can feel like you are communicating in different languages and things can get lost in translation.

SpIN boxes

Supporting autistic Special Interests (SpINs)

What you need:

- A small cardboard box or plastic box with a lid
- A range of special interest items

What to do:

1. Involve the child and parent/carer in putting together the SpIN box, adding favourite items, resources or provocations.

2. Ensure that it is in an accessible place for the child and that they feel a sense of ownership and autonomy when accessing the box.

3. To ensure that the SpIN box is child-led, let the child decide how and when the items are used and played with, and follow their lead when engaging in parallel activities or play.

Neurodiversity-affirming element

Actively planning and incorporating special interests reduces the stigma around repetitive and focused play, and normalises autistic traits.

What's in it for the children?

It is important to honour a child's special interests. Historically, this trait of autism has been viewed negatively with attempts to stop, divert or remove access to special interest play, as it is often considered restrictive. However, they are a valid aspect of autistic identity and can provide regulating and joyful experiences, which later act as a springboard for extended learning, development and growth. This activity can be useful for focused play, or for incorporating other activities and experiences including therapy or support sessions.

Taking it forward

- Other children may show an interest in SpIN boxes which is great. This is an opportunity to teach children about different traits and needs, and to encourage all children to think about their interests and hobbies.

Parallel play
Honouring neurodivergent styles of play

What you need:
- A range of toys

Definition

Parallel play, or 'body doubling', is a common play preference for neurodivergent children. Parallel play is when two or more individuals engage in different activities with each other while not trying to influence each other's space. It is a form of quality time and being 'alone together'.

What's in it for the children?

While it is important to pay observational attention to ensure that a child does not feel disconnected or isolated from others, it can also be enjoyable for a child to become immersed in their own play. As their play progresses, neurodivergent children can often prefer parallel play as opposed to cooperative play as too much intrusion can disrupt their flow. By choosing to play alongside, we can gently and respectfully connect with those children who play in different ways.

What to do:

1. Follow the child's lead and pay close attention to their play.
2. Sit alongside or nearby the child, leaving appropriate space so they can continue in their play.
3. Engage in your own play, or copy what the child is doing.
4. Show an interest in what they are doing, but do not intrude.
5. Embrace quality time, and if the child is comfortable, continue the experience.
6. Over time, the child will likely begin to welcome you into their play, for example, by offering a toy or by initiating communication.

Neurodiversity-affirming element

It has been suggested that parallel play is enjoyable for some neurodivergent children because it feels less pressured. Cooperative or busy peer play can be overwhelming with neurotypical expectations, information sharing and 'back and forth' processing which can take the joy out of the play.

✚ Health & Safety
Ensure that your environment facilitates solitary play and provides nooks, crannies and partitioning to reduce the play-skills overload.

Get outdoors

The outdoors as a remedy for sensory craving

What you need:

- Outdoor access

What to do:

1. Decide on a safe outdoor location, such as your nursery garden or a local forest area.

2. Carry out an environmental scan for possible sensory challenges, such as noise or busyness.

3. Carefully plan the transitions, such as travelling from nursery to the local park or getting ready to head outdoors. Perhaps consider inviting parents and carers along.

4. Follow the child's lead in the first instance and identify key interests.

5. Begin to offer provocations based on the interests children are showing outdoors.

Neurodiversity-affirming element

Being outside offers multiple benefits for neurodivergent children, especially with sensory-motor, emotional and social benefits. Things that may be difficult to achieve indoors become easier in less contained spaces. The fresh air, freedom and reduction of demands has a particular benefit for neurodivergent children. Behavioural issues such as fighting, moving and interrupting become less of a focal point in outdoor spaces. Research has found that educators also report less stress in supporting neurodivergent and disabled children when engaged in outdoor play.

What's in it for the children?

While the outdoor environment can present a whole heap of challenges for neurodivergent and disabled children, there are also a range of opportunities and benefits. Being outside has particular benefits for increasing opportunities for friendships, taking risks, experiencing success and achieving learning outcomes. While this idea might appear vague, it is hugely important to emphasise the sheer value of choosing to go outside.

Taking it forward

- Think about accessibility for a range of disabilities and how environmental barriers can be overcome to ensure outdoor play is an equitable opportunity.

Play mapping

Following children's interests

What you need:

- Clipboard
- Paper
- Coloured pens

Case Study

It has been observed that Haruto is quite fleeting in his play, appearing not to remain in spaces for too long. The key person decided to complete a play map to try to figure out which areas he was most drawn to, and why he may move between spaces. The play map showed that Haruto would frequently go to the small world area and play with the dinosaurs but would move away if the area became too loud or busy, often retreating to quieter corners and spaces and returning when the other children moved away. The key person interpreted this as the child feeling a little overwhelmed and decided to create some more partitioning in the space. She also set up a play box with dinosaurs that Haruto could transport to different spaces.

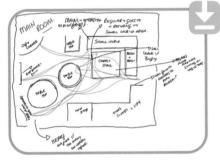

What's in it for the children?

Neurodivergent children's play can often be described as 'fleeting', meaning that they can appear to move quickly from place to place or not settle in one spot for very long. There are many reasons for this, including being movement-driven or in the exploratory stages of play. We often find it difficult to pin specific interests or play behaviours when this fleeting behaviour occurs. Play mapping enables us to follow the play flow and look for patterns.

Taking it forward

- Plan for children's play based on what has been found in the play mapping exercise.

What to do:

1. Draw a very basic bird's-eye view of the play space.
2. Allocate some time to pay observational attention to the fleeting play.
3. Using a clipboard and a piece of paper, use one colour to map the child's movements. When you repeat this mapping exercise, use a different colour to highlight the different mapping points.
4. Do this over several days, using a different coloured pen each time.
5. Review the play map at the end of the week and discuss your interpretations with the parents or carers.

Neurodiversity-affirming element

Play mapping serves many purposes, including finding out about interests, gaining an understanding of the child's sensory landscape, or considering whether the environment works well for the child.

Neuroinclusive now and next
A visual timetable to support predictability and familiarity

What you need:

- A small whiteboard or a laminated piece of card
- A whiteboard marker

What's in it for the children?

Now and next boards are relatively common in Early Years settings and are designed to support children with familiarity and what to expect. However, at times they can be misused as a compliance tool – for example, 'You must first do this, and then you can do that'. This is not how these types of visuals should be used. Now and next boards should provide rhythm and routines that help with motivation, understanding and predictability.

Taking it forward

- Increase autonomy by encouraging the child to make choices about what is 'now' and 'next' for them.

Top tip ⭐

The best way to utilise a now and next board is through free drawing or using basic symbols.

What to do:

1. Draw two boxes on a whiteboard or laminated card. Label the one 'now' and the other 'next'. You might also use the alternative phrasing of 'first' and 'then'.

2. Decide on a selection of symbols that you will use to represent activities, such as snack time, play, outdoors, toilet, nap time and so on. These can be built up over time as understanding grows,

3. Show the board to the child and point to each symbol individually. It is important to use very simple language – for example, 'Look, now it is breakfast, and next play.'

4. When the first activity has finished say, 'Breakfast has finished' (take the symbol off the board). 'Next it is play' (point to the play symbol).

Neurodiversity-affirming element

Neurodivergent and disabled children can experience thinking and memory differences. Processing lots of information can feel overwhelming, and retaining routine sequences can prove difficult. The now and next board breaks routines down into more manageable chunks so that the child can feel a sense of security and familiarity.

Ready, steady, blow

Building anticipation before attention

What you need:

- Bubbles

What to do:

1. Gather a group of children together.
2. Explain to the children that you have some bubbles that need to be blown away.
3. Blow the bubbles high into the air.
4. Shout, 'Ready, steady, BLOW!'

Neurodiversity-affirming element

There is often a demand on children's attention when developing speech, language and communication, but this idea can also be used to provide positive anticipation, and create fun and shared experiences.

What's in it for the children?

A common goal for neurodivergent and disabled children is to increase attention in adult-directed tasks. It is important to recognise that attentional control can differ between children. Often, the best way to build attention is through fun experiences, such as building anticipation, which later translates to attention. This activity can be incorporated generally into routines and is a fun way to develop skills in waiting and taking turns.

Taking it forward

The concept of ready, steady, go (RSG) can be used with a range of other props and can meet diverse needs including those with vision and hearing differences, for example:

- Using light-up toys, and using RSG for switching on and off.

- Building up a tower out of blocks, and knocking it down.

- Using puppets, and using RSG to perform a number of actions.

- Using pots and pans, or musical instruments, for noise making.

Visual pocket chart
Using visuals to support routines and understanding

What you need:

- Printed or hand-drawn activity cards
- A large piece of cardboard
- VELCRO® strips or double-sided sticky tape
- Plastic wallets
- A small basket

What to do:

This activity relates to a full day's routine. It will build the child's familiarity with what happens across the day.

1. Map out key activities and experiences across the day. Decide how each experience will be represented – for example, a sun for the morning, an apple for snack time and so on.
2. Create the visuals in any way you choose – for example, photographs, line drawing or symbols.
3. Identify an easily accessible space to display the routine.
4. Using the cardboard, create a long strip down or across the wall. Apply the VELCRO® or sticky tape.
5. Attach VELCRO® or sticky tape to your plastic wallets and attach these to the cardboard strip.
6. Place your routine visuals into the plastic wallets.
7. Place a basket at the bottom of the wall.
8. During the day, remove each visual once the routine is completed and place it in the basket.

Neurodiversity-affirming element

Visuals should never be used as a compliance tool. They guide and support autonomy, so always begin with child-led experiences. Children can be encouraged to engage with visuals and use them to communicate, but this must be through modelling and making visuals accessible and exciting, never through withholding attention or resources.

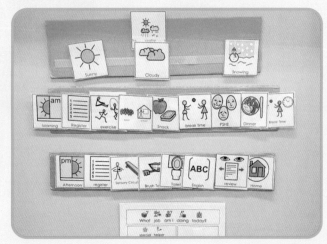

Definition

Augmentative and **alternative communication** encompasses the diverse ways children can access communication, particularly through non-speaking methods. Examples include the use of visuals, sign language or body language and technology which can aid a child when using their ways to communicate.

What's in it for the children?

Visuals are a valid and important form of communication and are particularly beneficial for children who have augmentative and alternative forms of communication; for example, if they are non-speaking or minimally speaking. Visuals are beneficial because they can be permanent, can increase autonomy and independence, reduce anxiety, enhance other forms of communication, and support with transitions and change.

Taking it forward

- Create multiple schedules and display them at eye level in different places throughout your setting.

- Promote generalisation by introducing visual supports gradually and build up a collection of various symbols and tasks.

Top tip ⭐

This routine can be used with a whole group or an individual child.

QR codes

Using technology in play and learning

What you need:

- A tablet, phone or portable smart device
- Access to a QR code generator

Top tip

Choose a Symbol Story by scanning the QR Code.

What to do:

- Support children to access books using QR codes that show the interactive or accessible version of the book.
- Visit the Stories with Symbols website (www.storieswithsymbols.com) for free videos of stories being read accompanied with communication symbols.
- Have an action rhyme wall with the QR codes so that children can choose the music they want to listen to and dance to.
- A QR treasure hunt encourages children to engage with different classroom areas. For example, stick up QR cards around the environment and ask children to find them and scan them.

Neurodiversity-affirming element

Embrace technology as a learning tool for neurodivergent and disabled children who have technology preferences.

What's in it for the children?

If you have children in your setting who prefer technology, you can use QR codes to engage them in new experiences, such as storytelling. While screen time should be appropriately managed, it is also crucial to remember that technology serves as a great learning and engagement tool for neurodivergent and disabled children.

Taking it forward

- For the home-learning link, you could create some resources for parents and carers to use at home with their children.

Declarative language
Reducing direct questioning

What you need:

- **No resources required**

Definition

Declarative language is based on making statements rather than asking lots of direct questions. It is the process of thinking out loud to cultivate at-ease reciprocal communication.

What's in it for the children?

Children are often faced with lots of commands and demands from adults. This can be overwhelming, particularly for those children who are neurodivergent. When expected to process lots of information, they can feel overloaded, making it difficult to engage, emotionally regulate and maintain attention. While we cannot eliminate instructions and commands, we can re-frame our language so that children have more time to process and respond.

Taking it forward

- Incorporate declarative language into your daily practice to help children to become autonomous, creative problem-solvers.

What to do:

To begin using declarative language, try to reduce direct questions or demands, and instead try the following:

1. Comment or make statements out loud about what you might be thinking, hearing, seeing, remembering or feeling.

2. Ponder aloud – for example, statements such as 'I wonder…' or 'Imagine if…' can provoke thinking.

3. Use flexible statements – for example, offer options and choices and different ways to respond.

4. Use your body language to demonstrate your thoughts and feelings and describe the process: 'It helps me to think when I…'

5. Maintain a low-demand approach so that the child does not feel pressured to provide a specific right or wrong answer. Declarative language is about a process of communication rather than a fixed answer.

Neurodiversity-affirming element

Declarative language can be used for a range of needs, including for those who may experience demand avoidance, have social or emotional differences or for those with different processing skills. It slows our communication down and allows us to be in the moment.

Declarative Language

Pondering "I wonder what would happen if...."	Commenting "Ahhhh I can see what you did there"	Imagining "Imagine if...."
Reflecting back "I saw what you did there...am I right in thinking..."	Explaining "Let's break this down..."	Connecting "Wow, this reminds me of...."
Admit when you get it wrong "I don't think I got that right..."	Possibility Thinking "remember that there is often always more than one answer or way of looking at things"	How to fail "Mistakes are learning and discoveries"
Silence	Process "Lets let our thinking sink in"	Action "let's act it out"

Mirror and model

Following the child's lead to cultivate communication

What you need:

- A quiet space in which to play alongside a child
- Toys related to the child's interests

Top tip ⭐

To maximise the connection built through mirroring, there must be recognition that children may feel intruded upon or we may interrupt their plans without meaning to. Signs of distress or irritation must be respected, and practitioners should step away so that they can work to find a time when the child is more receptive.

What to do:

1. Keep in mind that some children prefer solitary play, so you will need to be aware of the subtleties of interacting over interfering.

2. Sit alongside or opposite a child and begin to imitate their communication and actions. If it is within play, match the level of play, and limit your language. Avoid questioning during mirroring.

3. If there are signs of reciprocation or engagement, continue to mirror and show interest in the child's actions and behaviours. Over time, you will build personal knowledge of the reciprocated actions and their possible meanings.

4. As trust builds, introduce new actions, play or communication as a scaffold. Ensure you do this in the child's preferred communication.

Neurodiversity-affirming element

Mirroring is part of a wider intervention approach known as intensive interaction. This is when we imitate and reflect actions and behaviour back to the child to build a secure relationship, increase natural and spontaneous communication and increase social inclusion. Mirroring is also good for understanding the child's perspective and initiating shared experiences.

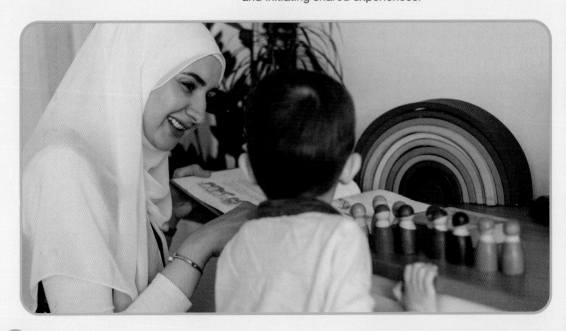

What's in it for the children?

Modelling is a common strategy, but we must first build trust and connection with a child. To do this, we can initially mirror their play and communication, which forms the foundations for later scaffolding and modelling.

Neurodivergent and disabled children will engage in many types of play, communication and behaviours, which can be seen as insignificant, especially if their actions appear repetitive or if we view everything as a 'symptom' of their neurotype or disability. Acknowledging and mirroring a child's play can build rapport, security and engagement. It is a way for us to let the child know that we see, hear and value them as they are.

Taking it forward

- Once you have built trust with the child, you can gradually begin to scaffold and model new skills.

Babble box

Using toys and objects to encourage chatter

What you need:

- A box with a lid
- Items that encourage the use of sounds and words, such as light-up items, toy animals, vehicles or blocks

What's in it for the children?

When children are acquiring language, it is important to provide time for them to experiment and play around with language. The babble box can be used to provide opportunities for a child to experiment with babble, sounds and words.

Taking it forward

- As you play, try increasing the words spoken. For example, you might say a word to describe the item as well as making the accompanying sound.

What to do:

1. You can choose to introduce the babble box during small-group play or with an individual child.

2. Fill the box with the items – for example a car, a farm animal and a building block.

3. Encourage the child to explore the babble box and vocalise the sounds – for example:
   - The cow goes 'mooooooo'.
   - The police car goes 'neee nawww, neee nawww'.
   - The building blocks fall down with a 'crash, bang, wallop'.

4. Provide pauses for the child to imitate.

Neurodiversity-affirming element

This is a low-demand way of having fun and experimenting with language. The range of items also means that children can choose which items to focus on, and this activity can combine adult-initiated and child-led play.

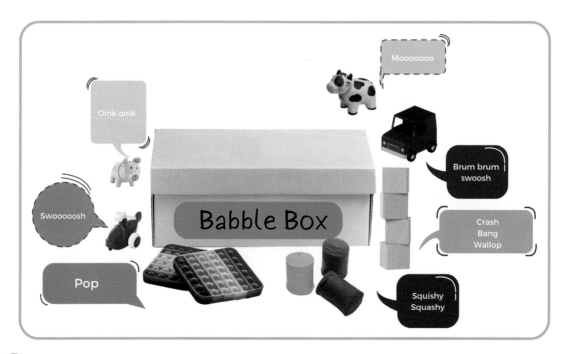

OREO
Observe, respond, exit and observe

What you need:

- **No resources required**

What's in it for the children?

Neurodivergent and disabled children are often accustomed to having their play interrupted for adult-led intentions, but we must develop a good balance so we do not interfere or overwhelm children. If practitioners are genuinely interested, authentic and natural, children will engage in more complex types of play, thus providing deeper learning. Children will also take risks, test ideas, develop emotional regulation and feel an increase in their confidence (Trawick-Smith, 2019).

Taking it forward

- Use observations to track how the child responded to your interactions. This will help you to understand what kind of interactions are valuable.

What to do:

1. Observe: Begin by observing the child from a distance. Think about whether they are immersed in solitary play, or if there are signs you are welcome to join their play. You will then need to decide how you might respond.

2. Respond: We often think 'respond' means to interact, but sometimes our response is to choose not to interact as we can see self-directed or peer-mediated learning. Alternatively, you may spot a need to scaffold or guide the learning. You may pose a question, provide a commentary, offer a possibility or solution, or ponder or offer to model and demonstrate. You may do this in a direct way, 'You could place this block here', or an indirect way, 'I think I will have a go'.

3. Exit: Take moments to step back out of the play so that the child can have opportunities for increasing autonomy.

4. Observe: Return to your observational skill.

Neurodiversity-affirming element

Many approaches for supporting neurodivergent and disabled children involve interference or redirecting play for neurotypical goals. The OREO idea empowers you to hold space for children to have autonomy within their play and interactions.

Embracing echolalia
Honouring autistic language processing

What you need:

- Play dictionary (see page 9)

Case Study

Robin uses delayed echolalia as a form of communication. His key phrases are "mom" and "go digging". His key person notices that the intonation is different each time he uses these phrases. Over time, and through observation she notices that saying "mom" is self-regulatory and used when he wants reassurance, and "go digging" is used to make requests and to express interests. The key person acknowledges these phrases and offers a response. Over time, he is experimenting with new phrases and chunks of language.

Definition

Delayed echolalia means the non-immediate use of utterances or words. For example, a child repeating a phrase they have heard which then becomes a familiar part of their language. This form of communication is considered part of Gestalt Language Processing, and is the process of learning language from 'whole to part'. The gestalts of any size are uttered but, over time, break down into smaller 'mitigated gestalts' which eventually become the literal single words. The language then gradually builds back up to include phrases and eventually grammatically meaningful sentences.

What to do:

1. Delayed echolalia can be a genuine attempt at communication, although it is not literal. We should be responsive and acknowledge the attempt.

2. During your observations, note down what the child utters in their personal play dictionary (see Play dictionary, page 9).

3. Delayed echolalia can serve many functions. Through your observations you might identify that the child is:

   - self-regulating, soothing or comforting themselves

   - making requests

   - answering questions

   - turn-taking

   - making declarations

   - giving yes/no answers

   - requesting

   - commenting

   - self-advocating.

4. Respond back to the child to acknowledge the echolalia, for example, by repeating or extending on what they have said.

Neurodiversity-affirming element

Gestalt Language Processing is a developing theory with much more to be understood, but an important starting point for Early Years educators is to acknowledge all types of communication. Focus less on questioning during the acknowledgement, try declarative language instead (see Declarative Language, page 23).

What's in it for the children?

If you were to conduct a quick internet search on delayed echolalia, you would disappointingly see some results that suggest that echolalia should be stopped, ignored or even punished. The ideas in this activity provide ways in which you can honour children's valid attempts at communication.

Taking it forward

- As you develop your understanding of delayed echolalia, you can begin to develop your practice across the four stages of Gestalt Language Processing. Accounts such as @meaningfulspeech and @bohospeechie are great examples for professional development.

Object of reference

Bringing communication and understanding to life

What you need:

- A range of objects relevant to the child's experiences
- VELCRO® strips

Definition

Objects of reference (OoR) are objects that can be used to represent an activity, person or place. We use them to help children to develop an understanding of spoken language. By using OoR, a child begins to link the word, object and activity together.

What to do:

- For anticipation: Become accustomed to using an object of reference (OoR) as part of your upcoming transitions – for example, showing a cup to indicate snack time.

- Sequencing: You can use OoR to show the sequence of events or a task. For example, showing a toilet roll followed by a hand wash to indicate what will happen when you go to the bathroom.

- Choices: During play, you may select a few toys that represent the different ways a child likes to play. For example, bricks for carpet play or a spade to indicate going outside.

- Labelling: For children who may not always feel confident in the environment, you may use the objects as external labels. For example, using VELCRO® strips to stick a car on the outside of a box of cars.

Neurodiversity-affirming element

Objects of reference can be used more generally or you can use them in personalised ways for individual children. Try to choose items that hold significance to the child. This won't always include functional items but instead objects that hold personal meaning. The end goal is for the child to use the OoR to communicate needs, so it becomes a form of reciprocal communication.

What's in it for the children?

Objects of reference are a useful starting point for building up understanding. The ideas in this activity provide ways in which you can utilise OoR into everyday practice.

Taking it forward

- As the child builds confidence, you may gradually move into visuals. For a while you may combine the object of reference and the visual, eventually relying more on the visuals or language.

Top tip ⭐

Start with a few objects, and keep it simple and consistent.

Wellbeing choice board

Supporting autonomy during emotional regulation

What you need:

- Card
- Marker pens
- Sticky tack, VELCRO® or magnetic sticky notes

What to do:

1. Note down examples of the co-regulation and self-regulation choices a child makes – for example, seeking out hugs when sad.
2. Create some visuals to signify the different choices.
3. When the child is dysregulated, use the board to guide the child to make a choice.

Neurodiversity-affirming element

This activity increases autonomy and choice for the child and recognises that children need different things at different times. The choice board builds a repertoire of self-regulation strategies and enables opt-in consent for different interactions in co-regulation.

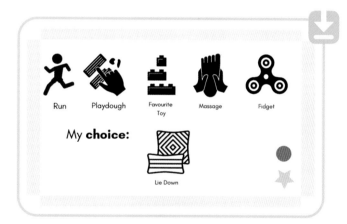

What's in it for the children?

Children need to have choices when engaging in co-regulation and self-regulation. However, children who are minimally verbal and non-speaking may need specific visual support to guide their choices. This idea is low-cost and easy to do and should be personalised for the child.

Taking it forward

- Set up the board for increasing independent use.
- Produce a wellbeing journal for the child.

Scented Playdough

When Hattie feels "fuzzy" with stress, she likes to take some of the scented playdough to play with. She tells me that this helps her to feel calm, and keeps her mind focused. We did this together and I taught her to knead the dough with her fists so she can really get rid of that fuzzy energy.

Hiding Space

Hattie told me that she likes to hide in the climbing frame when she is upset. She doesn't like to talk when is upset unless it is with one of her friends. When she feels this way, she can let me she wants to go there and I know she may just need some time to decompress. We added some of her favourite books there too so she can relax in that space when. we are outdoors..

Mood zones

Creating zones to support regulation

What you need:

- A piece of paper
- A pen

What to do:

Take a walk around your environment and draw a bird's-eye view of the space. Mark out the following:

1. A space to relax: This could be a reading space or a space that is specifically designed to support relaxation, such as a chill-out zone. Ask children about which colours they find calming.

2. A space to react: Our bodies have a right to react and therefore you should consider a space where children can regulate the residue of uncomfortable emotions such as anger, rage, sadness and frustration.

3. A space to retreat: Children need spaces to hide, such as dens, under desks and behind things. Nooks and crannies can be very beneficial for children who need to disengage to self-regulate.

4. A space to resolve: You and your entire environment offer the opportunity to resolve through responsive caregiving, empathy, forgiveness and role-modelling. Consider which spaces offer the opportunity for you to spend quality time with the children.

Neurodiversity-affirming element

Children self-regulate in different ways, and our environment can play a significant role in supporting wellbeing. By considering how we design the space, we increase autonomy for children to choose how and where to self-regulate.

What's in it for the children?

When children are accessing our Early Years' spaces, it is important that we recognise that the environment can influence emotions, behaviours and attitudes to learning, and so how we design the space must take into account different emotional states. This idea helps you to think about different zones for different moods, which can increase children's autonomy and independence in choosing how to self-regulate.

Taking it forward

- If you cannot have a designated zone for emotional regulation, consider how your environment can act as a third teacher, and incorporate self-regulation props across the space – for example, a fidget basket.

Reaction walls
Supporting mind and body connection

What you need:

- A display space
- A series of animal symbols or signs
- Feeling words on cards or a poster
- Action words on cards or a poster

What's in it for the children?

A reaction wall will help you to guide a child to match up their bodily sensations and emotions (interoception – see page 37) and can offer strategies for soothing and energising during co- and self-regulation. By knowing children's individual body maps of emotions, we are better equipped to identify what is happening to offer support, and to emotionally upskill the child.

Taking it forward

- Model describing your feelings and sensations. Narrating your interoception will help childen to develop a growing understanding. For example, 'My belly is rumbling, that must mean I am hungry.'

What to do:

1. If a child appears to be struggling to understand how they are feeling, use the reaction wall to guide them through.

2. Point to the different bodily sensations and name them. You could also use an emotions wheel to guide you.

3. Offer some suggestions of how the child might be feeling. For example, 'Do your body parts feel heavy? Could you be tired?'.

4. Offer a strategy to co- and self-regulate. For example, if the child says they are feeling buzzy like a bee, you could do some stretches or deep breathing.

Neurodiversity-affirming element

Children will experience a range of bodily sensations and it can take time to work out how these relate to their feelings. Taking time to explore body and mind connections supports emotional regulation and helps children feel better equipped in deciding which strategies work for them.

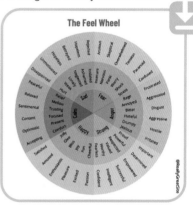

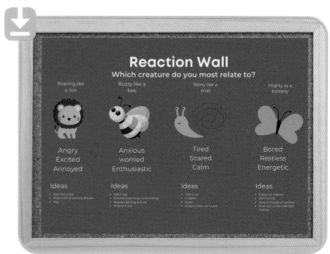

Transition bottles

To support with transitions

What you need:

- Cotton balls
- Essential oils
- A small plastic bottle with a lid

Top tip ★

Make a set of transition bottles that can also be used at home.

What to do:

1. Take a cotton ball and add 1–3 drops of essential oil.
2. Place the cotton ball into the small bottle, replacing the lid.
3. Add a label for the transition it will be associated with. For example, lavender for nap time and tea tree for toilet time or nappy change.
4. Before the planned transition, take the lid off the bottle and waft it near the child, letting them know what will be happening soon.

Neurodiversity-affirming element

This idea can be used with lots of different needs, including with children who have multi-sensory differences or for those who can become uncomfortable with transitions.

What's in it for the children?

Our sense of smell can be useful for supporting us with transitions and knowing what to expect when. For example, smelling food meaning it is time to eat, or the outside breeze indicating that we are going to go outside. Children are exposed to lots of changes during the day, and this idea can support and prepare for transitions that may make a child feel unsettled.

Taking it forward

- You can make smelly sachets that the child can carry in their pocket so they can continue to benefit from the therapeutic smells.

✚ Health & Safety

Always check which essential oils can be used with children and ensure that children are supervised.

Interobreathing

Short meditations to support regulation

What you need:

- No resources required

What to do:

Try the following breathing activities with the children:

1. **Dragon breathing:** Sit up straight, breathe in all the way, and breathe out like a fiery dragon. Draw attention to the heat of the breath.

2. **Bubble breathing:** Imagine you have a wand to blow bubbles, take in a deep breath through your nose, and slowly breathe out of your mouth to blow the biggest imaginary bubbles. Draw attention to the swooshing sound and stretching of the mouth.

3. **The flower and the candle:** Imagine you are holding a flower and a candle; smell the flower and then blow out the candle. Draw attention to the breeze in the nostrils and the possible smells.

4. **Soup breathing:** Imagine you are about to have a big hot bowl of soup; sniff the soup and blow the soup to cool it down. Draw attention to the taste buds and texture of the soup.

Neurodiversity-affirming element

Not all neurodivergent children will find mindful breathing beneficial as they may not register breathing sensations in the same way. Use clear language, and draw attention to focal points other than the breath. For example, talk about the heartbeat, describe movements or include deep pressure to emphasise the rhythm of the body.

Blow the biggest bubbles! How hard can you blow?

Sniff up the flower, and blow out the candle

Sniff the soup, and blow it to cool it down.

Breathe like a dragon. How hot is your breath?

Definition

Interoception means the awareness you have of your internal bodily states and sensations, including how biological cues and emotions physically feel in the body. For example, the sensation of warmth to indicate getting hot, or a racing heartbeat to suggest we are active or feeling stress. It is common for neurodivergent children to have interoceptive differences.

What's in it for the children?

Interobreathing focuses on noticing the changes and rhythms of our breathing. This idea can be used with children to emphasise interoceptive awareness or as a co-regulation activity when stressed or alert.

Taking it forward

- Add props to these breathing exercises to create more concrete ideas. For example, real bubbles or flowers from the garden.

- Change the breathing exercises based on a child's specific interests and preferences. For example, if a child loves dogs you might adapt 'dragon breathing' to 'woof breathing'.

The Flower & The Candle Meditation

What we want to ensure for all children is that they can use strategies to manage their own feelings. This meditation experience is useful when children become stressed or worried, and helps to regulate and calm their breathing.

1. Ask the child to imagine that they have a flower in one hand, and a candle in the other.
2. Suggest thay they sniff up the flower, hold their breath for a moment, and then blow out the candle.
3. Repeat for as many times as desired.
4. The next time the child becomes upset, remind them of this technqiue so that theu can recognise moments of stress and respond to them.
5. It is also important to talk to children about what stress may feel like so that they understand why their breathing becomes busy.

Wellbeing dice
Building up self-regulation knowledge

What you need:

- Medium-sized dice with side pockets, or a homemade dice box made from a small cardboard box
- Felt-tip pens
- Thick card

What to do:

1. Draw examples of self-regulation skills, such as having a lie down, on each of the cards.

2. Place them into the dice slots, or draw them directly onto your dice box.

3. Either one-to-one with a child or in small groups, throw the dice so that the children can see the different self-regulation skills.

4. Encourage the children to use the dice when they are feeling dysregulated and are unsure what to do.

Neurodiversity-affirming element

This activity recognises that children need different things at different times to support their wellbeing, rather than feeding into 'one size fits all'.

What's in it for the children?

When you are working with young children, you will be helping to build a repertoire of self-regulation and wellbeing strategies. The wellbeing dice activity is a great way to try new ideas, is fun and provides choice.

Taking it forward

- Support the children to design their own wellbeing cards and to use the dice independently.

Sensory den
A low-cost way to support escape and retreat

What you need:

- A very large cardboard box
- Gaffer tape
- Scissors
- A cushion
- A blanket

What's in it for the children?

During the day, you will find that there are children who may need to escape from the main environment or who need time to retreat from others. While cosy corners can be lovely, other children often occupy them. It may also be costly to invest in separate sensory spaces or resources. You can, however, make a low-cost sensory den quite easily.

Taking it forward

- Encourage the children to decorate their sensory den or add additional sensory elements such as glow-in-the-dark stars or a touchy-feely wall.

What to do:

1. Decide on a location for your sensory den.
2. Open up the cardboard box. Ideally, it will be large enough to fit a small child.
3. Tape the top and bottom shut so that it is secure.
4. Cut out a large circle on one side of the box and strengthen the opening with gaffer tape.
5. Place a cushion and blanket inside.

Neurodiversity-affirming element

There are moments throughout the day when children like to retreat and escape from adults and other children. Many neurodivergent children have to process lots of information across the day, and this can be overwhelming. Having dens to go and hide in can offer the perfect sensory relief.

Sitting still soothers

Reducing sedentary behaviours

What you need:

- No resources required

What's in it for the children?

There may be times during the day when children need to sit – for example, during circle time. This should only ever be for short durations, and it is important to provide children with sensory stimulation so that they do not become too sedentary. This set of soothing ideas can be taught to children to utilise when sitting, in order to maintain engagement and comfort.

Taking it forward

- Encourage the children to utilise these soothers across routines and rhythms of the day.

What to do:

Demonstrate the following soothing strategies to children:

- Sit on your hands for weighted support.
- Rub your hands together as if you are trying to warm yourself up.
- Place your hand over your heart; take a deep breath and tune into your heartbeat.
- Lift yourself slightly off your chair for chair push-ups.
- Give yourself a giant hug by wrapping your arms around yourself and squeezing.
- Squeeze and release your fists.

Neurodiversity-affirming element

Neurodivergent and disabled children often show their attention and listening in different ways and need to move to engage. These ideas affirm the need to move and show children that there is no requirement for them to sit still for long periods, which can negatively affect learning.

SOS bag
Saving your senses with personalised items

What you need:

- A small bag or bumbag
- A selection of toys, such as bubbles and fidget toys
- Personalised items that mean something to the child, such as a favourite toy car

What's in it for the children?

Early Years environments can be overwhelming, especially for neurodivergent children who are hypersensitive or hyposensitive to sensory aspects of their environment. Toys centred around sensory soothing, fidgeting, or a child's special interest can help facilitate self-stimulatory behaviour (stimming) to help children regulate.

Taking it forward

- Once the child recognises the bag and its function, they can be involved in choosing what should be kept inside.

What to do:

1. Set up a bag with a range of sensory resources to be kept continuously accessible.

2. Gradually adjust resources to meet the needs of the child by paying attention to their interests and which sensory experiences they seek.

Neurodiversity-affirming element

An SOS bag that is consistently available provides a sense of security and increases children's independence in recognising and responding to their own emotions. Equally, it can be used by the practitioner to provide comfort and acknowledge the child's feelings in an unobtrusive way.

Top tip ⭐

Encourage parents and carers to create an SOS bag that can be used by the child at home.

Homemade lava lamp

Creating visual calming aids

What you need:

- A clear container with a lid, such as a plastic bottle
- Water
- Vegetable or baby oil
- Food colouring
- Glitter
- An effervescent tablet

What's in it for the children?

This homemade lava lamp activity can be a great way to meet sensory seeking needs, and can be done alongside the child.

Taking it forward

- Use tonic water if you want to make a glow-up lava lamp.

➕ **Health & Safety**
Ensure that the tablets are handled by the practitioner only and that they are stored safely before and after use.

What to do:

1. Fill your container a third of the way full with water.
2. Add the vegetable oil to just near the top of the container.
3. Add a few drops of food colouring and some sprinkles of glitter.
4. Break the effervescent tablet into pieces and add to the liquid, one after the other, creating a lava lamp reaction.
5. Replace the lid while the tablet settles.
6. Add more tablets when wanting to make the bottle more reactive.

Neurodiversity-affirming element

This is a low-cost and fun activity to do alongside the child, offering sensory soothing.

Touch book

Bringing stories to life using the senses

What you need:

- A hole punch
- A5 cardboard
- Child-safe glue
- A range of textured materials, such as fabric, feathers and buttons
- An A5 ring binder or string

What to do:

1. Hole punch the number of pieces of card you need.
2. Glue each of the chosen textures or materials to a separate piece of card.
3. Place the card within the ring binder or bind together using the string.

Neurodiversity-affirming element

Sensory books can be used with children who have visual differences, are blind or who have sensory processing differences.

What's in it for the children?

There is no greater sensory experience than simply touching the 'stuff' around you, but some children may be reluctant to engage in lots of sensory exploration. Children should never be forced to engage in sensory exploration to increase their tolerance of an item. However, you can offer sensory provocations for children to explore and to build their awareness of different textures and patterns.

Taking it forward

- Introduce touchy feely dice which can be purchased or made.
- Add a few drops of essential oil to the material for scent.
- Make touch books based on popular stories, such as *We're Going on a Bear Hunt*.

Top tip ⭐

Head to craft shops to look for offcuts or to ask for donations.

Back-to-back breathing
Building interoceptive awareness

What you need:
- A comfortable space to sit

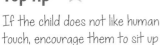

Top tip ⭐

If the child does not like human touch, encourage them to sit up against a wall or big cushion. .

What's in it for the children?

Often neurodivergence, especially autism, can impact the way touch is processed, making typical attempts to soothe through physical contact ineffective. Back-to-back breathing eliminates eye contact and soft touch and provides a predictable rhythm, thus bypassing some potential barriers to typical physical comfort. It is a safe and comfortable way of offering support during dysregulation.

Taking it forward

Suggest other tactile-based activities such as:

- hand massaging
- using a soft bristle brush to try skin brushing
- tapping parts of the body where there is tension
- squeezing and relaxing of hands
- lying down with legs lifted to release tension and anxiety.

➕ **Health & Safety**
Do keep in mind children's comfort levels about activities involving touch and bodily autonomy. Always ensure you ask for consent, and supervise for signs of discomfort.

What to do:

1. Put the children into pairs or ask them to choose a partner. Invite them to sit on the floor back-to-back.

2. Ask them to sit up tall and to close their eyes if they would like to. Ask them to start to breathe in through their noses and out through their mouths.

3. Encourage the children to focus on breathing together at the same time.

Neurodiversity-affirming element

Touch can have a calming effect and alter the way stress is handled, thereby promoting mental and physical health.

Sensory shows
Demonstrating sensory sequences for calming and regulation

What you need:
- Aluminium kitchen foil
- Popping candy
- Water in a spray bottle or a jug of water
- Bubbles

What to do:
1. Roll out the aluminium foil in a straight line, describing what you are doing as you go.
2. Pour the popping candy along the aluminium foil.
3. Gently pour the water over the popping candy and wait for the candy to snap, crackle and pop.
4. Blow bubbles over the popping candy creating a further visual element.

Neurodiversity-affirming element
This activity offers sensory soothing elements, and can help build anticipation and attention.

What's in it for the children?
At times, watching a sensory show in action can be soothing and regulating, with the added advantage that it can be relatively low-cost. This idea is one that can be used as an end-of-day circle time activity or at any point when children are winding down. It aims to be a low-arousal activity and so is perfect on days that have been busy or overwhelming. You can also create video demonstrations so that parents and carers can also try this activity out at home.

Taking it forward
- Try creating different sensory shows by using trays and combining paint colours.

Top tip ⭐
When you have finished the activity, swill the popping candy off the aluminium foil and pop it in the recycling.

Homemade sound baths

Using sound to support calm spaces and minds

What you need:

- Chimes, a sound ball or gong, or a playlist featuring musical instruments

What's in it for the children?

Music and sound is a core feature in early childhood settings and supports physical and emotional wellbeing, as well as being a pleasurable experience. While it is common to hear nursery rhymes in our Early Years spaces, the use of sound baths is less common. However, sound baths have the potential to offer calming benefits for children and are a lovely co-regulation experience. The practice of sound bathing, as the name suggests, is the practice of being immersed in sound for calm and relaxation.

Taking it forward

- Empower the children to autonomously access the instruments and resources to create their own sound bath routines.

- Ensure that you consider individual needs when sound bathing, such as a child's sensory needs or triggers, or if a child has hearing differences or difficulties.

What to do:

This activity can be delivered as a guided meditation with children, or they can explore the instruments and create their own sound bath.

1. Find a calm space and turn the lights down or off.

2. Create sounds using the instruments or by playing the soundtrack whilst providing calming affirmations for the children, such as 'I am safe' and 'I feel calm'.

3. Continue the activity for 5–10 minutes, but ensure that the children are able to opt out when they have had enough.

Neurodiversity-affirming element

This activity can regulate breathing, create a sense of calm and cultivate a sense of 'being in the moment'. It can also provide an effective transitional activity.

Energy breaks
Supporting busy minds and bodies

What you need:

- Card
- A pen
- Lollipop sticks
- Sticky tape

What's in it for the children?

Movement is a critical part of children's experiences and is beneficial for the development of gross and fine motor skills, along with sensory processing, language, communication, self-regulation and positive self-identity. Movement is also vital for thinking skills. However, too often children are expected to be still. This is harmful to all children, but particularly neurodivergent and disabled children who often rely on movement to engage.

Taking it forward

- Encourage the children to choose their own energy breaks and add them to the cards.

What to do:

1. Decide on a range of alerting and soothing energy breaks that can be incorporated across the day, including:
   - dancing and high-energy play, such as jogging really fast on the spot
   - self-tickling – for example, stroking your arms or palms
   - rhythmic actions, such as jumping and rocking
   - singing to favourite songs.

2. Draw pictures of each of the energy breaks on the cards.

3. Stick the lollipop sticks to the back of the cards and use them as visualisations to accompany the breaks.

Neurodiversity-affirming element

Exercise shapes our bones, lungs and muscles, but it also helps to develop our brains. In fact, movement develops structures within our brains which helps with the develoment of our thinking skills. Keeping our children active helps to increase oxygen to their bodies which is required for optimal brain function. So, regularly adding short movement breaks into the day energises children and helps them to feel well regulated. Physical activity helps the brain to become engaged and ready to learn!

Visual soothers

Reducing visual noise in times of emotional and sensory discomfort

What you need:

- Sensory craving items, such as fidget tools
- Green items, such as plants
- Access to natural light or lamps
- Items to furnish, such as cushions and drapes

Definition

Visual noise is any visual stimulus that impacts your focus, attention or wellbeing. For example, a brightly lit environment with many posters on the wall is likely to be overstimulating. We can become easily overwhelmed when there are many competing visual noises.

What's in it for the children?

We need to be aware of visual triggers in the environment, particularly for children who have sensory differences. These ideas can be used in the moment to reduce any visual overload. So much focus is placed on environmental aesthetics, but we need deeper explorations of the impact of environmental triggers in the learning environment, such as visual noise.

What to do:

- **Turn off bright lights:** Prolonged exposure to strip lighting can lead to headaches, increased negative energy, dehydration and fatigue.
- **Reduce window displays:** Seeing green spaces is crucial for children's wellbeing in order for them to be able to see the real world. Window displays, although often used well, can make children feel contained and trapped. If you do not have direct access to green space, you can add plants.
- **Fidgets:** Children often benefit from having items to fidget with to focus. Have fidget baskets dotted around your space. Also consider how some children fidget in different ways, such as swinging their legs when sat on chairs. Support this by having resistance bands on the legs of chairs.
- **Colour balance:** Spaces are often either intense with colour or too beige – balanced is best. We can have an intentional use of colour, for example, by adding neutral items such as cushions or drapes or having naturally backed boards. We can use colour to set the scene.
- **Displays:** Avoid hanging displays that can be distracting for children and can contribute to feelings of being contained. Create displays that are dynamic and at the child's level. Other possibilities include creating a portfolio for children to flick through, or creating exhibition spaces to exhibit their work.

Neurodiversity-affirming element

It is important to recognise that there will be sensory joys and triggers – children respond differently to visual noise, so it is about understanding their individual profiles.

Moving with materials
Using Lycra® for deep pressure and resistance

What you need:
- Two metres of Lycra®

Top tip ⭐
Ask parents and carers for offcuts and donations.

What's in it for the children?
Lycra® is a great sensory tool as it is stretchy and offers resistance and deep pressure. It can support sensory integration, sensory craving and builds proprioceptive skills (coordination of body parts).

Taking it forward
- If you are able to sew, the Lycra® can be turned into a body sock or tunnel. Step-by-step instructions can be found online.

✚ Health & Safety
It is essential to supervise any play with Lycra®. Carry out a risk assessment and supervise the children at all times, and ensure that you check in with the child for consent before any activities involving resistance with materials.

What to do:
- **Child-led play:** Make Lycra® available as a provocation and observe the ways in which a child utilises the material.

- **Sushi roll:** Open the Lycra® on the floor and encourage the child to lie on top. Roll the fabric around the lower half of their body and invite them to roll back out of the material.

- **Butterfly wings:** It is important that this activity is risk assessed and the child understands they do not have to crouch under the material. Guide the child to crouch and to hold the material at the corners around themselves. After you say 'ready, steady, go', encourage the child to break out of their cocoon and to become a butterfly. This idea is perfect for the outdoors where the elements, such as wind, create resistance.

- **Tug of war:** For co-regulation, play a tug of stretchy war by pulling at either end of the material.

- **Drape:** Use the Lycra® as a drape in nooks and crannies to provide a quiet space for the children.

Neurodiversity-affirming element
Some children can feel physically and emotionally out of tune with their bodies. The use of materials and movement can help connect emotions and bodily sensations, which can feel soothing and calming.

Actions over answers
Supporting impulsive engagement

What you need:
- No resources required

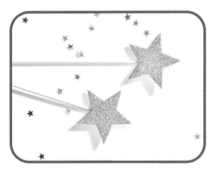

What's in it for the children?

A common concern from educators is when children have impulsive engagement – for example, shouting out or interrupting, or having difficulty waiting for a turn. This can be viewed as disruptive behaviour, but is usually a sign of eagerness to join in. Children who are neurodivergent, such as those with ADHD traits, are often driven by impulses including excitement. This idea helps you to think of novel ways to support impulsive engagement.

Taking it forward

- To ensure children engage in planned activities and experiences, consider the following components: interest, challenge, novelty and urgency.

What to do:

- **Whisper and pass the answer along:** When asking questions or wanting contributions from children, ask them beforehand to prepare to whisper the answer to the person next to them and pass the answer along.

- **Shout it out:** Children are accustomed to being told to be quiet or to lower their volume, but it is also beneficial to encourage children to engage with different volume levels, including being able to shout out the answer or their thoughts. This idea also builds anticipation. Incorporate 'shouting out' into circle time or adult-led group activities.

- **Turn-taking props:** Sometimes it can be helpful to provide children with a talking prop so that they can symbolically and visually process turn-taking. Using novelty props during circle time, such as a wand, talking stick or talking teddy, can be useful.

- **Show me/go find me/copy me/this or that:** You can involve active learning when children are contributing ideas during group activities. Getting them to engage in movement or to provide prompts can support processing.

Neurodiversity-affirming element

If you find yourself giving children lots of behavioural reminders without changing your expectations, you are unlikely to see much improvement particularly because, for some children, impulsive engagement is a trait of their neurodivergence. Offering dynamic ways to answer or contribute helps to meet a broader range of needs.

Heavy work basket

Supporting autonomy during sensory integration

What you need:

- A medium-sized basket, such as a laundry basket
- Play dough
- Paint rollers
- Blocks
- A fabric door stop
- Resistance bands

What's in it for the children?

All children are building their skills of proprioception (coordination), and for some children this may be an area where further opportunities are needed to cultivate and maintain this skill. For other children, they may have lifelong proprioceptive difficulties and may benefit from heavy work to feel a sense of grounding.

Taking it forward

- Heavy work items do not need to be expensive or purchased. Go on a heavy work hunt across your setting or home or ask for donations from parents and carers. As long as you risk assess, most items can easily be utilised.

- To support individual needs, you may develop a basket to be specifically used by one child.

What to do:

1. Set your basket up somewhere in your environment and explain to the children that, each day, you will add an item to the basket and demonstrate how to use the item to support with their emotions and feelings.

2. Each day, select an item and demonstrate its use. For example, kneading play dough, or doing weights with the door stop.

3. Ensure that the basket is available and accessible in the environment.

4. Rotate the items to keep children intrigued and engaged in returning to the basket

Neurodiversity-affirming element

When a child hasn't fully developed 'mind free' movement (unconscious body awareness), they can feel quite out of sync with the world, and this can cause feelings of anxiety and disorientation. The use of a heavy work basket empowers the child to try out different ideas autonomously and can be used for self-selection. In addition, all children can benefit from the basket and engage in shared experiences.

Definition

Heavy work is defined as any type of activity that pushes, pulls or creates resistance within the body. Heavy work aims to support the sense of proprioception, which helps our body and brain work together to understand and navigate space and objects.

Fidget Items

Heavy work routines
Honouring sensory processing differences during the day

What you need:

- Heavy items, such as large cardboard boxes and laundry baskets
- Space to move

What's in it for the children?

There are general routines that can be built into everyday experiences to support proprioceptive awareness, including deep pressure and stress relieving movements. If you sense that a child is feeling restless or overwhelmed, offering heavy work routines can support alerting and calming bodily states.

Taking it forward

- Invite the children to make their own choices of how to self-regulate.
- Utilise heavy work play across the day and through your routines, for example, by lifting weighty items, cleaning the tables with cloths or stacking books.

What to do:

When you spot a child is restless or overwhelmed, try the following:

- Encourage the child to place both palms up against the wall and place feet slightly apart. Invite them to lean into their palms and press hard. Add challenges, for example, ask them to roar like a lion.

- Encourage the child to massage their hands together. You can also add props such as massage balls.

- Encourage the child to push another child in a large cardboard box or to push a laundry basket filled with items.

- Encourage the child to give themselves a big bear hug by wrapping their arms around their body and squeezing. Add challenges, for example, 'Can you tap your fingers on your back as you squeeze?' or 'Give yourself a compliment.'.

Neurodiversity-affirming element

This idea recognises that children need sensory integration opportunities throughout the day and equips the child with self-regulatory strategies.

Balloon volleyball

Building balance and coordination skills

What you need:

- **Balloons**

What to do:

1. Standing up, or on your knees, hold the balloon in your hands and let the child know that you are going to throw the balloon to them.

2. Throw the balloon up into the air and hit it with both of your hands towards the child, encouraging them to hit the balloon back to you.

3. Keep hitting the balloon back and forth, trying not to let it float to the ground.

Neurodiversity-affirming element

This activity strengthens the child's core muscles, improves balance and encourages coordination. In addition, it can be done indoors or outdoors depending on the child's preference, and builds focus and attention.

What's in it for the children?

Balloons have a wealth of therapeutic benefits. They can be great for vestibular input and help children with sensory integration (the way children process the things they experience through sensations such as light, touch and sound). They can be used for fun games that require children to use their muscles, joints and coordination to transport the balloon. Do be mindful of the child's sensory preferences before introducing this activity – for example, a sensitivity to the scratchy sensation of the balloon.

Taking it forward

- Encourage peer bonding by asking a group of children to stand in a row and pass the balloon backwards to each other over their heads.

Pom-pom sweep
Shared experiences for shared attention

What you need:

- Washi tape
- Pom-poms
- A hand brush

What to do:

1. Using the washi tape, create a square on the floor or at a table.

2. Place all of the pom-poms outside the square of tape.

3. Using the hand brush, encourage the children to take turns to brush the pom-poms into the centre of the square as fast as they can.

Neurodiversity-affirming element

This activity provides a range of benefits whilst also being fun. It is a good activity to do together, creating anticipation and excitement as you try to brush the pom-poms. It is also great as a pre-literacy activity which builds fine motor skills. You can create different shapes with the washi tape, and set challenges with the activity so that the children can sweep in different ways.

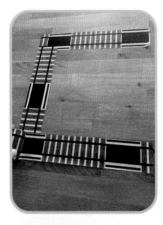
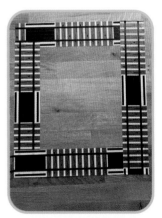

What's in it for the children?

This is a low-cost activity that can encourage a shared and fun experience between adults and children, or between peers. It can be set up as a provocation and can be used to develop children's anticipation. While in the most part the practitioner will follow the child's lead, there will also be activities that are practitioner-led and can build attention and focus.

Taking it forward

- Reduce the size of the square so that the children have to manoeuvre the pom-poms into a smaller space.

Chunking
Ensuring information is accessible

What you need:

- Visuals or objects of reference to support verbal instructions

Top tip ⭐

Often, the advice with instructions and information is to slow down, but sometimes we can go too slowly. Be flexible with your pace of language and adapt it for individual children's needs.

What's in it for the children?

Chunking is the act of breaking down a task, communication or instructions into smaller 'chunks'. This makes the information more manageable and therefore easier to process. This approach takes the pressure off a child when they feel overwhelmed by demands.

What to do:

1. Identify an activity a child needs support with – for example, preparing to go outside.

2. Decide on the tasks they will need to do to go outside, such as fetching their coat.

3. Provide the instructions but break them down – for example, 'Let's head to the coat pegs'. Wait until they have completed the action.

4. Leave a pause and then add the next instruction, 'Find your picture on the peg'. Pause again giving the child time to process the information.

5. Focus on one thing at a time and provide praise and encouragement as each chunk is achieved.

6. Make time for practice and try not to berate when a child is unable to process the chunked information.

7. Limit language for instructions to reduce complexity.

8. Give plenty of processing time and avoid reprimanding a child if they are not quick to act or respond.

9. Try to be specific in your descriptions and be prepared to model or demonstrate what you are saying.

10. Be prepared to repeat!

Neurodiversity-affirming element

Neurodivergent and disabled children often require more time to process information. By empowering a child with more time to process, we create a greater number of opportunities for them to succeed in tasks.

Backwards chaining
Building competence in new skills

What you need:

- A jigsaw puzzle

Definition

Backwards chaining refers to breaking down the steps of a task and teaching them in reverse order. This gives the child a greater sense of accomplishment and builds confidence. The aim is for you, the adult, to do less and less while the child does more and more, always ending with the child being able to do all stages independently, having developed the skill.

What to do:

1. The first time you introduce the jigsaw puzzle to the child, place all but one piece of the puzzle together on the ground or on a table. Encourage the child to place the last piece in the puzzle.

2. When the child places the last piece, provide meaningful praise, such as 'Wow, look, you did it!'.

3. As the child becomes confident placing the final piece, take a reverse step and place all but two pieces of the puzzle together. Encourage the child to place the last two pieces.

4. Repeat this reverse step until the child can complete the full jigsaw puzzle.

5. Provide plenty of encouragement and praise.

Neurodiversity-affirming element

There may be occupational or play skills that the child is building confidence with. When they are unable to complete a task, this can knock their confidence. By using backwards chaining, we build up a child's confidence and provide positive feedback so that they remain motivated to give things a go.

What's in it for the children?

Backwards chaining helps the child to develop new skills in a non-pressured way. It breaks down tasks so that they become more manageable. It also encourages us as adults to be mindful of some of the complex steps involved in developing new skills.

Taking it forward

- Make a list of tasks that involve sequences so that you can build backwards chaining into your children's everyday routines.

- You might also try forwards chaining which can also be beneficial in building new skills. Forward chaining involves teaching the child to initially complete the first step of a task before gradually building up to the full task.

Chair warm ups
Support with comfortable sitting

What you need:

- Chairs

What's in it for the children?

There will be times across the day when children may be expected to focus or to follow adult-led instructions. Building warm-ups into children's routines can help regulate their minds and bodies and prepare them for periods of sitting or paying attention.

Taking it forward

- Encourage the children to make their own choices of how to regulate. For example, they may find a particular warm-up beneficial or enjoyable.

- For those children who find sitting difficult, provide cushions, exercise balls and opportunities to sit in different positions other than upright and facing forward.

✚ Health & Safety

Ensure that you risk assess for this activity and provide supervision. Children will need to be supported to understand how to keep safe when using a chair for things other than sitting.

What to do:

Explain to the children that they are going to do some warm-up exercises to get them ready for learning/the day.

1. **Chair press:** Invite the children to place their palms onto the seat of the chair and do three press-ups.

2. **Take your leg for a walk:** Ask the children to place their hands on the back of a chair for support and raise their left leg up, holding it in that position for five seconds before lowering it back to the floor. Invite the children to repeat this action with their right leg.

3. **Around the world:** Invite the children to sit in their chairs and to gently rotate their heads to the left for five rounds. Encourage the children to repeat this action a second time, towards the right.

4. **Baby bear:** Whilst the children are sat in their chairs, invite them to lean forward and place their heads in their laps.

Neurodiversity-affirming element

Sedentary behaviour (being still) can have detrimental effects on long-term development, so where possible movement should be incorporated into activities that require the child to be seated.

Theraputty play

Supporting sensory seeking input

What you need:

- 2 cups of plain flour
- 2 tablespoons of vegetable oil
- ½ cup of salt
- 2 tablespoons of cream of tartar
- Up to 1 ½ half cups of just-boiled water
- Food colouring, glitter or essential oil (optional)
- Large mixing bowl
- Wooden spoon

What's in it for the children?

Theraputty is often used as sensory support for children who are developing their fine motor skills, strength and fine-gross motor control. It also provides deep-pressure play (see Moving with materials, page 49). Theraputty can be used in many ways, but initially it should be introduced as a provocation during child-led play.

Taking it forward

- Encourage the children to roll the putty into different shapes, such as balls, pancakes and sausages.
- Support the children to use the putty as a stress reliever by squeezing, pinching and pressing.

What to do:

1. Mix the dry ingredients and vegetable oil in a large mixing bowl.
2. Add the food colouring, glitter or essential oil (if using) to the just-boiled water.
3. Gradually add the water into the mixing bowl until the ingredients come together.
4. Once the mixture has cooled, invite the children to help knead the putty until the stickiness is gone.

Neurodiversity-affirming element

Theraputty has a range of benefits. It can be used as a sensory soother or fidget tool, and adding essential oils creates scented theraputty. It is beneficial for building up hand and finger muscles and is a great literacy activity.

Top tip ⭐

The theraputty can be used during adult-directed activities as a self-regulating fidget.

✚ Health & Safety
Carry out a risk assessment prior to the activity. Always supervise children carefully when near to hot water.

Digital technology
Utilising technology to understand children's learning and engagement

What you need:

- A recording device, such as a tablet
- A means of watching the recording

What to do:

Videoing can be used in the following ways:

1. Set up a recording device, such as a tablet, when a child is at play.

2. Record the child for a short period of time. Alternatively, let the child use the device to decide what they wish to record.

3. Watch the video back with the child to generate an opportunity for the child to observe their own play, to communicate about it, and to offer feedback about their play.

Neurodiversity-affirming element

For many neurodivergent and disabled children, technology is a crucial learning tool. It can be used in dynamic ways to understand children's play and learning, as well as a teaching and modelling tool.

What's in it for the children?

Videoing has been used in autism support previously, and was first introduced in the 1980s as a way to support autistic children with life skills. However, it can be used in other dynamic ways. Using videos of the child or children engaging in play and learning can be great for watching back and helping a child to understand how they might do things, their strengths, and areas where they might need further help.

Taking it forward

- Create dual language videos for children who speak multiple languages so instructions can be given in a more familiar language.

- Provide technology to children and encourage them to take pictures or videos of their favourite toys or spaces to play. This will provide you with an insight into the child's perspective.

Neuroinclusive stories
To support all children's understanding of neurodiversity

What you need:
- Access to a computer software, such as PowerPoint, Pages or Word
- Access to clip art

Definition

Terra Vance, the founder of Neuroclastic, a website for empowering autistic voices, introduced the concept of **neuroinclusive stories**. According to Vance, neuroinclusive stories are for anyone, regardless of whether they are disabled or not, to help all people navigate differences in a way that embraces inclusion and diversity.

What's in it for the children?

Neuroinclusive stories are for anyone, regardless of whether they are neurodivergent or not, as they help all people navigate differences in a way that embraces inclusion and diversity. Neuroinclusive stories can help children to understand their differences, or they can be used to introduce concepts and ideas about different disabilities and forms of neurodivergence.

Taking it forward
- Ask the children for their ideas on topics they would like to learn about, making it child-centred and child-led.

What to do:
1. Identify a specific trait, situation or experience that you want to teach the child about.

2. Create a story, for example, about why some children like to line things up, using PowerPoint. Alternatively, access a template at www.eyfs4me.com.

3. Ensure accessibility by including symbols, such as clip art or line drawings, within the story for non-speaking or minimally speaking children.

4. Share the story with the group during circle time or during small group opportunities.

Neurodiversity-affirming element

The joy of a neuroinclusive story is that it can be personalised and made relevant to the cohort of children you are working with. For example, one educator wanted her children to understand why children may have different equipment for their physical needs and created her own story, which included the children as characters. This enabled the children to make connections with their real-world experiences.

Sensory stories

Bringing stories to life through movement and the senses

What you need:

- A story, such as *Look Up* by Nathan Bryan

- Props related to the story, such as aluminium foil, things that light up or space dust (glitter)

Definition

A **sensory story** is one that serves to activate each of the senses to encourage engagement in a variety of learning situations. These range from simple engagement to knowledge recall, memory, communication, vocabulary development, social skills, literacy, movement and so on. Each has a different purpose. This may be to calm, to share experiences, or purely to encourage attention or interaction.

What's in it for the children?

Sensory stories can have a range of uses, including developing imagination, introducing new concepts or life skills, sensory immersion or experiential learning. They can be adapted to suit a range of needs.

Taking it forward

- Encourage children to act out their own stories and to utilise props.

What to do:

1. Choose a story that links to a child's interests or fascinations.

2. Decide on the key take aways and select a few ideas, words or sentences that relate to these. It is best to keep them short and simple.

3. Read the story to the child using the props to bring the story to life.

4. Create suspense by introducing different aspects of the story and encourage engagement from the child through noise, rhyming and movement. Repetition is key here.

Neurodiversity-affirming element

Sensory stories can be used for a range of needs including visual, hearing differences, sensory processing, and for increasing engagement in literacy.

Top tip ⭐

There are many guides online for developing sensory stories. For example, Joanna Grace, who is an autistic occupational therapist, has written a number of books on sensory stories.

Symbol stories

Ensure increasing accessibility within books

What you need:

- A storybook, such as *We're Going on a Bear Hunt* by Michael Rosen
- White card
- A pencil
- Scissors
- Double-sided sticky tape

What to do:

1. Decide on the book that you will share with the child.
2. Read through the book and either choose a selection of symbols that are relevant to the story using a visual system such as Widgit©, or hand-draw the symbols on white card.
3. Produce a label for the front cover of the book.
4. Cut out and stick the symbols to the pages of the story.
5. Share the story with the child. Draw the child's attention to key concepts and ideas.

Neurodiversity-affirming element

This activity increases accessibility by providing an additional way to engage with the same story as the rest of the class, thus meeting a broader range of access needs.

What's in it for the children?

For children who use visual symbols or who may use augmentative and alternative communication in the longer term, it is important to consider how our resources can be made accessible. A storybook with words may be difficult to follow, and incorporating some symbols throughout the book can increase accessibility.

Taking it forward

- Visit the following website for Widgit© story packs and books: www.widgit.com/resources/stories/index.htm.

LOOKING FOR BEARS

Symbol Story

looking | bears | outside

Glossary and References

References

Milton, D.E. (2012), 'On the ontological status of autism: The 'double empathy problem''. *Disability & Society*, 27, (6), 883–887.

Trawick-Smith, J. (2019), *Young Children's Play: Development, Disabilities, and Diversity.* New York: Routledge.

Glossary

Ableism	Discrimination against disabled people based on the assumption that non-disabled people are inherently superior.
Divergent pathway	Development that is different from typical milestones.
Neurodivergent	Having a mind that functions in ways that diverge from what society typically defines as 'normal' or typical. For example, being autistic or dyslexic. Neurodivergent children are often viewed through a deficit lens of problems, impairments and delays.
Neurodiversity	The diversity of human minds and the biological fact that human brains and minds differ from each other.
Neurodiversity-affirming practice	The ways in which we affirm, accept and presume competence in children who are neurodivergent or disabled.
Neurodiversity-informed practice	Practice underpinned by an understanding of neurodiversity and developmental differences.
Neurodiversity paradigm	A paradigm is a perspective or set of ideas. The neurodiversity paradigm rejects the deficit lens and perceives brain differences as a biological fact and valuable, meaning there is no 'normal' or right brain. The neurodiversity paradigm advocates that all humans and all minds have unique potential.
Neurotype	The type of brain a person has in terms of how they interpret and respond to different aspects of the world.
Neurotypical	Having a mind that functions in a way that aligns with the social construction of 'normal' or typical. Our educational frameworks are predominately designed for children who present as neurotypical.
Traits	Shared elements of a neurodivergence or other disability. The use of trait is to move away from 'symptom' as linking factors are not always negative, and so over-pathologising can have a negative impact.

50 fantastic ideas for supporting neurodiversity